Circling the Sunset

114 haiku and senryu

Maurice Tasnier

First published 2005 by IRON Press
5 Marden Terrace, Cullercoats,
North Shields, Northumberland
NE30 4PD, England
Tel/Fax: +44 (0) 191 253 1901
Email: seaboy@freenetname.co.uk
www.ironpress.co.uk

ISBN 0 906228 59 X

© Maurice Tasnier 2005

Typeset in Garamond 11 pt
Pagesetting, layout and cover design by Kate Jones

Printed by Field Print, Boldon, Tyne and Wear

IRON Press is a member of Independent Northern Publishers

IRON Press books are distributed by Central Books
and represented by Inpress Ltd, Northumberland House,
11 The Pavement, Pope's Lane, Ealing, London W5 4NG
Tel: +44 (0)20 8832 7464
Fax: +44 (0)20 8832 7465
Email: stephanie@inpressbooks.co.uk
www.inpressbooks.co.uk

Photo: Maggie Dane

Maurice Tasnier has had his poetry published in nine countries since the late '50s but did not start writing haiku until 1997. His first haiku collection, *From the Ninth Star on the Left* (Snapshot Press, 2000), said by one reviewer to be 'bitterly funny', has twice been re-printed. After many years as an evening newspaper sub-editor and a morning paper TV critic, he pursued a social work career until his retirement in 1996. Married with three children, he describes himself as a 'long-serving grandad', and lives at the seaside in Somerset.

By the same author

From the Ninth Star on the Left
(Snapshot Press 2000, Third Impression 2001).

Acknowledgements are due to the editors and publishers of the following publications (in the UK unless otherwise indicated) in which many of these poems originally appeared:

Aabye, Acorn (USA), *Blithe Spirit, Crinkled Sunshine* (Haiku Society of America Members' Anthology 2000), *Flat* (British Haiku Society Members' Anthology 2001), *Frogpond* (USA), *Haiku* (Croatia), *HQ Poetry Magazine, Intersections* (HSA Members' Anthology 1999), *Modern Haiku* (USA), *The Omnibus Anthology* (Hub Editions 2001), *Other* (BHS Members' Anthology 2004), *Presence*, RAW NerVZ (Canada), *Snapshots, still, Time Haiku, Voices and Echoes* (HSA Members' Anthology 2001).

Awards: *grandma's album* - 2nd prize, Haiku Presence Award 2001, *those words* - 2nd prize, Haiku Presence Award 2000, *missing the trip* - runner-up, Millennium Haiku Calendar Competition 1999 (Snapshot Press), *the doorbell...* - winner (October), *pallid sunshine* and *late autumn* - runners-up, Haiku Calendar Competition 2001 (Snapshot Press), *reading the story* - Peace Museum Award, 33rd A-Bomb Memorial Day Haiku Meeting, Kyoto, Japan, 1999.

Contents

Saving Sins	7
Taking Breaths	13
Chewing Walls	19
Skirting Daffodils	27
Colouring Cheeks	35
Wobbling Chairs	41
Clicking Shut	47

Saving Sins

hell-fire sermon
  the preacher pauses to wipe
  a watery eye

good mornings exchanged
her gardener asks *do you
have Jesus in your life?*

we all seem
extra friendly today -
lesbian pair's blessing

salvation army
hymns stirring
the park trees

the priest's
muttered absolution...
summer waiting

hushed church...
receiving the host he
swallows the wrong way

fervent choir...
I don't envy
Him

priest's duty visit...
the only warmth is from
our cat in his lap

Sunday drizzle
  faintly from next door
  the old ladies' hymns

as the bombs drop
a vicar suggests
prayers for peace

reassuring...
there's always *someone* sick
to pray for

confessional...
the little boy saves
his worst sin for next time

Maurice Tasnier

Quaker silence...
the flowers also
sitting there

Taking Breaths

joining with
the dawn chorus
my smoker's cough

walking to post
your letter   I ache for you...
sciatica

my first visit to
the osteopath...the creaking
of a chair

looking so much
younger than me
the hairs on my leg

chance meeting
   old friends exchange
   new misfortunes

ice pack on my leg
   nobody but me
   to ogle that thigh

waiting room leaflet
how to help your doctor
I pretend to read it

memory loss
   her eyes look around
   for the words

recalling the days
it sounded like a flower...
dementia

clinic waiting room...
slumped in a corner chair
old magazines

the coolness
on my arm
a nurse's hand

a speeding sequence
of ceiling lights and corners –
view from the stretcher

deep breath for me please
(yes nurse I'm doing it...
for *you*)

pictures from
the scanner - I just
don't know myself

darkened ward
   the voice still asking
where am I?

cardiac rehab group –
she tells us the story of
her arthritis

so much medication
all I will leave
are side-effects

Chewing Walls

grandma's album
  over the pressed sunflower
  a small hand hovers

peeling a tangerine
  its exposed fruit
  a perfect fit

a few cross words...
I re-arrange
the window cacti

poking my head round
the curtain   eye to eye
with a robin

this nice lady staying
so now I can't say
shit
    naturally

watching attentively
but not understanding
    my cat

our eyes meet –
I catch the sound
of a silent miaow

stormy exchange...
we fall silent for
the weather forecast

a carving slip
  father bleeds
  on the beef

screeching seagulls
helping to keep
Sunday afternoon awake

keeping to the lines
between the patio slabs
emerging ants

gazing deep
into the fuschia   more
and more flowers

into the straggling
clematis a dragonfly's
pointed precision

number engaged
　her droning on
　to someone else

Picasso flower
my four-year-old could do that...
　　then why didn't he?

these nice visitors
　I retreat to the bathroom
　and fart

somewhere in
all the talk and laughter
a small shudder

the meal over...
sipping liqueurs we watch
the Paschendale slaughter

those words
in her final letter
everywhere   craneflies

darkening close
to the long funeral day
  halo of the moon

having the last word
as the kettle boils
and drowns it

her week away...
the choice of places
in the dishwasher

my evening shadow
now alone
chews on the kitchen wall

Skirting Daffodils

first warmth...
the colours of
distant rooftops

squall long past
　the shelter deckchair still
　flat on its back

Easter morning -
our cat attacks
its new neighbour

June evening
　the blackbird too shrill
　for my hearing aid

missing the trip
to his favourite pub...
Father's Day

mid-afternoon
　eyes closed to the sun
　I dream sky

high summer heat
　shifting to make room for
　her irritation

between funerals
the vicar checks
the cricket scores

damp holiday streets
  smell of the sea
      with chips

pallid sunshine...
a tortoise skirts the edge
of the tree's shadow

on the cropped lawn
   eating grapes
    seedless

summer remains
playing on the patio
the fuschia's shadow

waiting for
our visitors
  rain...

late autumn
  along the tree's bark
  crinkled sunshine

the doorbell...
a giggle
of little witches

All Saints' Day
  closing the garage door
  on old shadows

cold moon
  a wind gathers the garden
  into itself

penny for the guy –
reaching into my pocket
the cold wind

a growing snowdrift
  all around it
  the drained sky

lengthening winter...
the white emptiness
of the hospital bed

shortest day
　not even pausing
　at the cemetery gate

Colouring Cheeks

her second look –
I adjust my face
from a grin to a smile

outside chapel
lovers sharing
the gift of tongues

sipping pale sherry
her words
colour my cheeks

she wants me
to look in her thigh?
I check my hearing aid

her unfolding my fantasy flowers

as she licks
the chocolate from her finger
I dribble

her fingertips
saliva silkened
tremble my lip

warmly
rapt
in
her
thighs

at the toll road
her hand in my pocket
takes its toll

love play
  reciting her parts
    my hands

ruminating on
the zeal of my mouth
  her tongue

dressed again...
just as though it
never happened

pledging eternal love
she checks her watch

a long silence
  turning away she
  hugs herself

across a crowded room
our eyes
don't meet

Wobbling Chairs

from the old
park bandstand
a cider belch

a walk in the woods
   even saying hello
   to the man with no dog

school gate
   mothers unravelling
   a tangle of children

Kielder Water ferry...
the crunching sound
of grandad's crisps

Maurice Tasnier

small town arts ball
   the bank manager's wife
   with a permanent smirk

my mistake –
starting to say sorry
to the cash point machine

a punctured tyre
   looked at from every angle
     still flat

deep in thought
or perhaps not
he picks his nose

all her troubles...
by my third pint
I am so understanding

first letter home
  he checks the spelling
  of diarrhoea

the car sales girl
just can't believe my age –
    I buy it!

assertiveness class
  the newcomer
  re-arranges the chairs

care plan meeting
the Down's girl asks each in turn
*and how old are **you**?*

the funeral over
we each take home a cigar
from his last box

poetry reading...
the chair in front of mine
has a wobble

to the newscaster:
and I hope *you also*
have a great weekend

Clicking Shut

a leafy suburb
   the down-and-out
   on his way out

reading the story
of the leper's healing
a hibakusha*

refugee girl
with her new dress
her old eyes

left behind
   the clouds
   behind the clouds

---

*survivor(s) of the Hiroshima or Nagasaki atomic bombs, August 1945

a scant breeze
the faint sound
of gregorian chant

walking the trail...
already a trodden daisy
starting to unfold

a glassful of water
   holding
   its coolness

empty moment...
the garage door
doesn't quite click shut

blank sheet
 a lone gull
  circles the sunset

Maurice Tasnier